JOURNAL OF EMOTIONS

JUDITH K JACOBS

What is a poem but emotions?

Words of strength, weakness,

love, laughter or sorrow.

A soul in print from beginning

To end.

Dreams of a lifetime; a role

created,

a role played.

DEDICATIONS

Judith Kay Jacobs was born in Bemidji, Minnesota on March 14, 1942. The family moved to Fergus Falls, Minnesota in 1945. Judy began reading at five years old. She began writing At 23 and is still writing At 82. Judy has worked in many capacities at Grace United Methodist Church plus enjoying music as a handbell soloist. She was also church secretary at St. James' Episcopal Church for 16 years. In between, she enlisted in the U.S. Army and is a veteran.

Judy and her late husband, Franklin, had four children: Bethany, Todd, Jeff and Sue plus many grandchildren: Kayla, Mariah, Alex; grandchildren Keagan, Jasmine, Ava, Maddie, Alexus and Blade, to whom this book is dedicated.

Imagine

Who is the stranger? You or me?

> *Come, reflect with me, at least we'll try to discuss the world and love.*

Well, the world and lack of... yet give me a date, a time, a year...

> *There is much to say, the time is near!*

We watch more hate than love I see -

> *Gibberish! It's not too late for me! I'll change their minds with kindness too...*

I know I can't, I know it's you. You're the Master, I'm sure you see -

> *Love is my King! Life is a play! We'll discuss this again another day.*

LIFE IS FOR THE LIVING

*Life is for the living
and life you'll find in death.
Life is in the sunlight's ray
and the warm, warm baby's breath.
Life is in God's outstretched arms
when hope seems far from you.
But in His gentleness and strength
love will come pouring through.
Love is anticipation.
Expect the best each day.*
When the mountain looks much higher,
then you'll stop to pray.

Going Home...

With a wave and a laugh, you whirl out the door-

how could we know we would see you no more?

You came to be with us in joy and in pride,

He sent you with love to be at our side.

We watched you grow tall and reach out to care

for life and for others, and He knew you were there.

You ran through the fields with a twirl and a shout -

when Father reached out to bring you about...

He has new fields to roam, He has brought you home.

With tears in His eyes, He acknowledges pain.

His tears fell so heavily we thought it was rain.

Such a joy you have been, we loved you so much,

but He loved you too, and He reached out to touch...

He has given us laughter, though heartbreak is here.

He has given us love; we feel you are near.

With a wave and a laugh and a swing of your hair

you have gone to join Him and will wait for us there.

{This was written for a friend whose 16-year-old daughter was killed on a highway on her first day of driving her car...it went everywhere, and they put it in her funeral} The school asked permission to put it in their yearbook. Unfortunately, I did not have a chance to edit.

A Gift

A precious thing is the human touch.
It becomes a beginning and an end.
May it impose upon your mind
the image of a friend.
A touch that calls us to concern
and lets us feel what pain employs,
it does not take for granted
but communicates both love and joy.
We are sometimes tempted to refrain
ourselves and look the other way
while in the distance we hear a cry
and realize what our heartaches say.
We reach to God for love so boundless,
this undeniable love He gives,
that we may pass it on to others
for in each of us this touch can live.
Another thing we should not forget
though we are each other's friend,
yet we struggle and are set aside...
we need the human touch to survive.

THE ARTIST

The artist's brush was dipped in snow.
Across the rooftops it did go
creating ridges white then gray -
it is not night; it isx not day.
From the house the brush glides down
to pile snow high all around
the streets, the skating rink and park,
and children playing after dark.
Suddenly the bristles flew and came up
dripping brown, dark blue
to make trees spring from ground so cold.
streetlights reflecting silver and gold.
The artist, before his canvas now,
pauses and smiles at memories recalled.

TO LOVE...

Your mouth on mine is so sweet,

like honeysuckle and dew.

Our thoughts do meld, our hearts do beat,

and I love your eyes so blue

as they open in gentle surprise...

I sense your wonder, I do.

Is love simple, moving, deep?

Am I with you as you sleep?

We see eternity as above

when I grasp your hand, your heart, your love.

For through whatever great endeavor

your haunting of me will be forever.

I Wonder... (Another thought)

Understanding yourself is a great accomplishment.

Understanding someone else is an even greater accomplishment.

Regardless of who we are or where we come from, this gift is yours.

I cannot give it to you for you already have it.

Keep it with you always and use it often.

Reaching out to others is a part of you and me

and we will hold it close to our heart.

MY LAND

I took over our family farm...my home!

I will never leave it.

The fields I worked, sometimes by hand

sometimes by plow...My land! My land!

Golden wheat drying in the sun.

Flocks of geese flying in the fall.

Plowing through winter snow to find the lost cow...

My land! My land! A lifetime on this land.

A leather lined face for my love,

trees lining my path home.

FALL

The harvest moon hangs like a gold coin in a darkened sky,
mirrored in a pond of glass.
Naked branches push upward, silhouetted against its hue,
resting on grass of burnt sienna.
Fields harbor brown-mottled corn stalks with
corn cobs holding their own in the first light of day.
Warm weather of the season past turns away
as cool weather's time has come together with a light rain
embracing treetops tipped with frost.
Winter is waiting for spring to make its appearance
in the early morning mist.
The sun rises in remembrance.

TO LOVE

Come into my mind, love.
Come in there and see
the making of the feelings
I've built it for you and me.
See into my lovely mind,
into my eyes so clear.
See exactly what I think,
how love can be a mirror.

A Dream...

If you open your eyes in the still of the night

seeing nothing because of darkness not light,

sensing your heartbeat even and calm

while your thoughts, half asleep

wander through and repeat the music...a dream?

flowing into a stream...

A ray of light finds its way through a window

casting shadows about and you know you are able

to dance in soft light - a ballet if you wish...

pirouetting in time, almost missing in space

as the darkness grows faint, the sun taking its place.

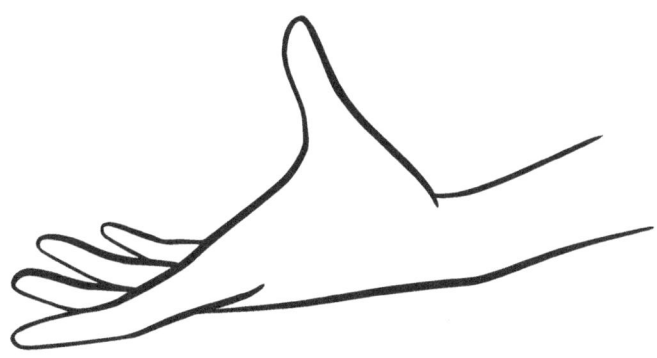

FALL

I walked this morning in the chilled air,

the coldness not striking hard

but enough to feel winter trying to force its way in.

It is Fall, with colors taking over reluctant trees;

leaves falling endlessly, ever so graceful

onto a ground not yet cold, still warm with life.

Feel the air. Breathe. A deep breath...deeper...

I take into myself a freshness so exhilarating;

morning dew and wood burning in the distance.

The wind gives a gentle push forcing its

strength to encircle trees - wailing around buildings.

I want it to never end, this kind of peace.

I would walk forever.

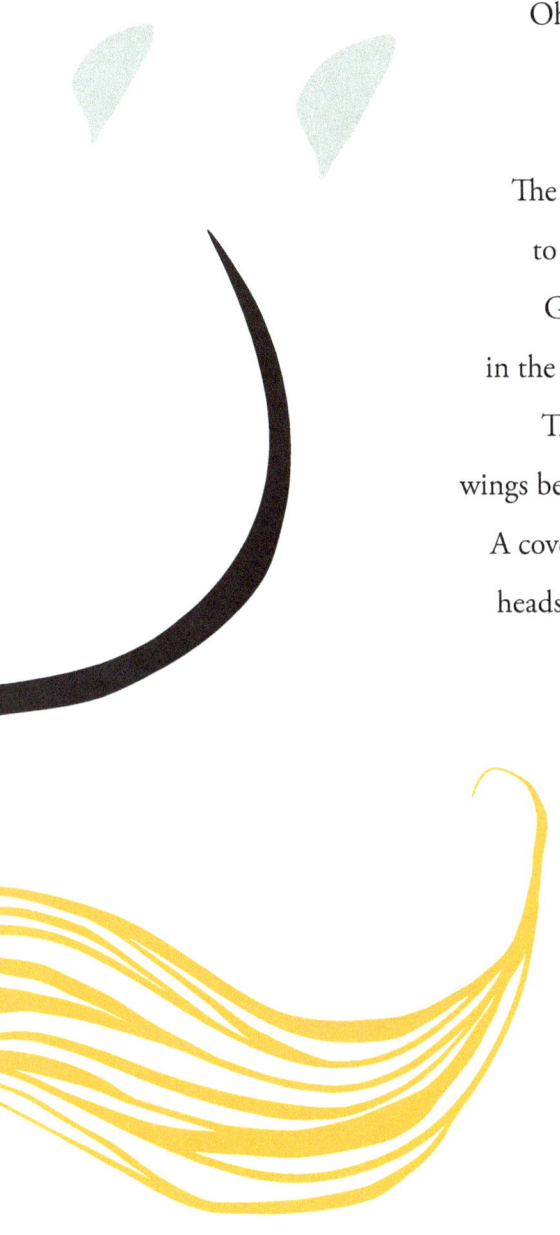

Oh, should I find a nice Fall day
where the sun beats down
and children play.
The leaves are looking for a breeze
to find a place to hide and tease.
Geese fly to their feeding place,
in the fields and playing with mates.
The ducks will in formation go,
wings beat the sky-night havens know.
A covey of quail the north will find;
heads underwing...hunters be kind!

SCHOOL DAZE

So, you don't want to go to school?
Don't want to learn that Golden Rule?
You'd rather stay at home in bed
and not face the things you dread.
I don't blame you, but you see
everyone would be mad at me
if I ignore the scholars great
and let you be so very late
at learning all the things you should…
I would not feel very good.
Because of love, not hate I guess
you'll maybe learn and not regress.
It is important not to roam
so maybe you will write a poem.

DAUGHTER

You are not so very tall,

but as a beauty - wow!

Eyes so large with lashes long

and your voice can sing a song.

One so sweet so nice I fear

to look too long, to disappear!

You are so quiet, yet I see

an inner spirit moving me.

Waves

Waves.

washing away years of sand

made into castles by small hands -

impressions of footprints of small feet,

of bodies covering the nearly invisible grains.

Waves.

Striking upward with white caps reaching out

to finger a tree washed away from its homeland,

dancing forward to feel rough stones

lying silently in the moonlight.

Waves.

Reaching hearts...flowing over our emotions.

KITES

Remember the kite you flew high in the sky?

With all your might you pulled that string -

holding tight, you ran so quick!

The wind was strong, your voice grew thick

from calling to the kite..."Stay up! Stay up!"

The joy to see it. The joy of remembering it.

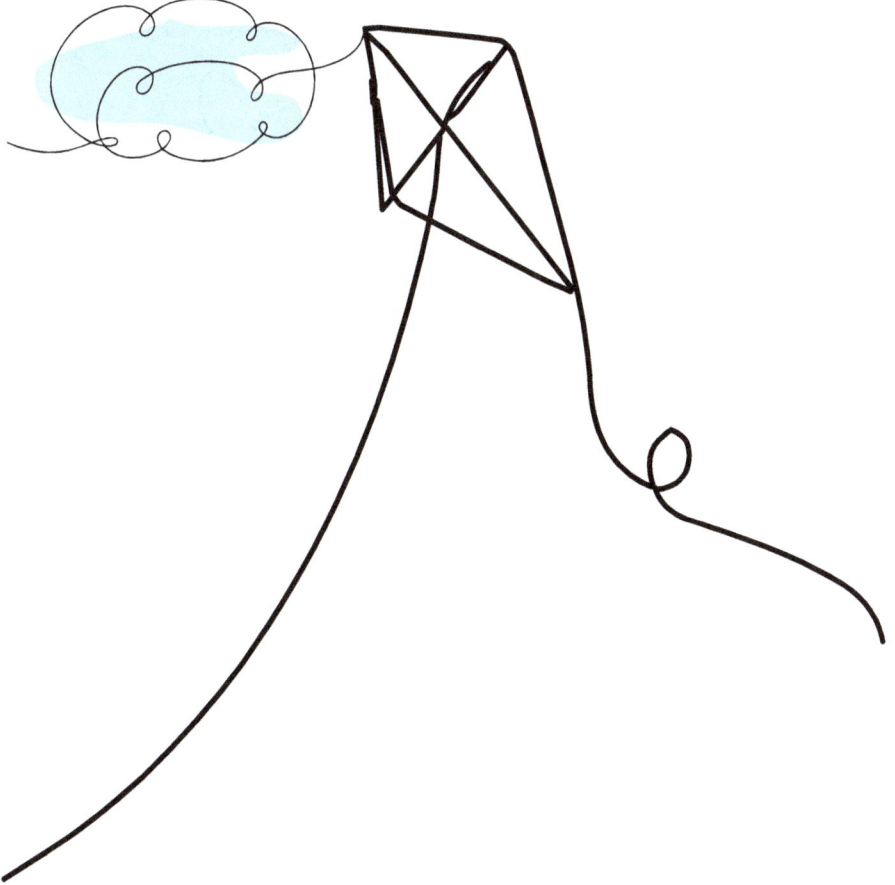

NEW LOVE

See the girl cross-legged there? A baby facing her?

She leans back to look at him...pulls his hands to take a look,

the little face an open book all sincere as life begins,

a simple charm of what has been.

With his face between her hands, she looks into his eyes.

He looks at her, seeing her and happily he sighs.

All the signs of love are there, her eyes are fairly glowing

at the beauty of this child, a life, all hers is growing.

FRIENDS

Walking down a dusty road with a special friend,

watching seasons come and go, moving 'round the bend...

Sharing all our problems that seem to come along,

sharing life's adventures while listening to birds in song.

Sensing joy and happiness, or just being there

or sharing an umbrella and showing that we care.

Like a sunset will always be there, this friendship will always last,

and as that winding road goes on, we'll think often of the past.

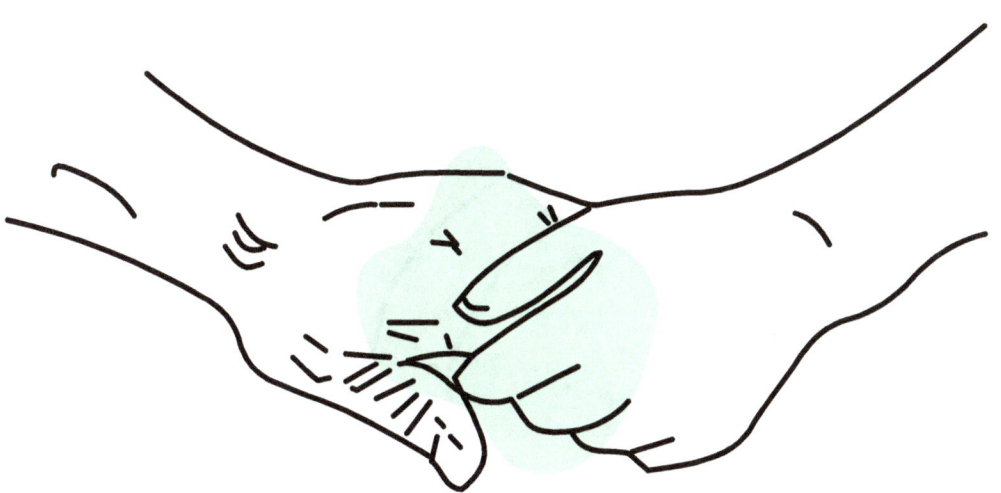

LOVE

Softly, softly eyes alight

with a joy, suppressed delight

at the beauty that beholds me;

rapture, glories that engulf me.

Moving slowly by the firelight,

open arms caressing gently

searching for the splendors sent me.

FOREVER

Mary sat on a rock. She ran her hand over its smoothness, its coolness in the sunset of evening.

Her mind wandered – an angel came to her? A baby named Jesus. She felt overwhelmed. Still, she knew he was there, he moved within her, maybe to calm her. She saw Joseph coming, a shadow in the sun.

Joseph was so good to her, so loving. The baby moved again. Joseph held out his hand to help her up and smiled at her.

They would do this together.
Hand-in-hand they walked down the path toward home with Jesus.

An Open Door

It's Easter.

As church bells began to ring

the congregation began to sing.

Across the street on a grassy hill

three small children sat so still.

The big church doors were open wide.

Beautiful people went inside.

Soon, something else was clear

a heavenly smell drew the children nearby.

They were walking inside when

a tall man asked, "Where are you going?

This is God's house..." They cried in fear.

They ran home but did not tell their mother.

They were afraid they would get in trouble.

There was no food, or anything more

so, they went up the hill to watch the door

when a man in black walked up to them,

"Come with me, it's cold out here.

This is Jesus' house. He wants everyone nearby.

Please come in, we have food for you,

and take something home for your mother, too."

They did.

THE MIST

The mist comes to foliage nearly engulfing it,
moving gradually up to the treetops.
The droplets of water move across lakes and streams
enclosing a Loon in the process,
the shadow of a fish jumping in the air.
The mist moves into the city,
to the top of skyscrapers and
nearly blocking the flag of red, white and blue.
People walk through the mist,
some with umbrellas, some with arms crossed
from the dampness of early morning.

LOVE

All the love I can give you,
all the love I can feel
is coming from my soul;
emotions not quite real.

Let it lock within your spirit.
Let it work your body through
covering you with its essence
as my life pours into you.

SUN

The earth rejoiced as the sun came up
to move between the trees.
A body of water on the old lake
moved slightly in a breeze.
Tall grass is reborn feeling warmth
as geese fly into camp.
I sat on a log watching the scene,
my dog resting on my lap.

Night

What should I think?
O God, my Father
as the day falls to the eve.
You've come in dreams throughout the ages
in happiness and grief.
You can read me all too easily
while I toss and turn toward morn.
Vague thoughts interrupt me
and I walk close to the thorn.
I'm awake as dawn arises,
pray the prayer you once did.
This prayer reconciles me
with tears to do your bid.
Father, may your Spirit find me
in your arms, your mind, your will,
as my soul and being come together,
and I am still.

SEPTEMBER

new season

early fog

cool mornings

serene sun

empty nests

deer browse

leaves fly

sleeping grass...

Enjoy it!

Leaving

I left the earth today.
I remembered how to sing.
A rose-colored sky on my left...
I could see it.
A sunset of bright gold
and flashes of purple -
red blazing across the sky,
silhouetting everything
down below in simplicity.
I left the earth today
remembering childhood
and I run, longing for what?
Now, I'm home!

Well...

An old lady fell over right on her head.
She had such a headache she went back to bed.
She later got up and looked at the moon,
grabbed her old witch hat and her favorite broom.
She unlocked the door and ran to the shed,
grabbed a black cape, got out a balloon
and flew right away to the Man in the Moon.
That didn't help her, so she flew down the street
throwing candy at kids who thought she was neat.
At this point she thought she'd better go home,
so, she flew through the woods, and hung up her hat,
stuck her broom in a closet and told it to, "Stay!"
Halloween is over! But you know I'll be back.

(Oh well. What can I say...Judy)

MY LOVE

Though you are a thousand miles away,

I feel your presence every day.

The morning sun shines from above,

your spirit is here, it speaks of love.

Love. A reason to be giving.

Love. A vision I am living.

Do you feel it like I do?

The strongest thoughts pull me through.

The longest day I've ever spent

is waiting for you to relent...

wanting you to hold me tight.

Love. A word we should not fight.

LOST

I am in the forest looking for you.

Your love is here. You are not.

I sat under a canopy of trees for a long time

gazing at the stars, thinking of you.

You are far more lovely than the scenery of nature.

If you were here, I wouldn't see anything but you.

I would have held you in my arms all night long

looking at you the way I love to do.

Give your heart to me, love.

TO A SINGER

Your eyes intense upon the camera,
glowing with a tender love
for the song you are singing;
hearts beat fast...wings of a dove.

Your voice is soft, slowly rising,
hands moving in emotion, too.
Audience hushed, not even breathing -
carry them away with you.

Body young and so enticing
wrapped in clothing made of silk.
Feel the earth and ocean's rising
for a song of love you built,

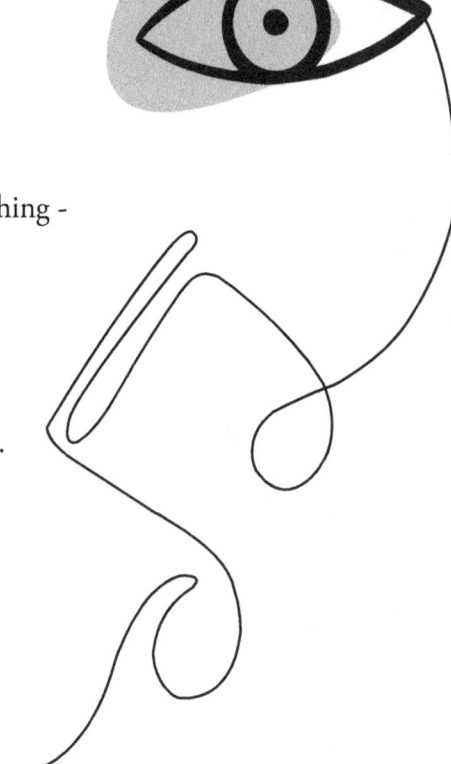

A Beginning...

The sunset came and so did Jesus,
born to us on earth.
Angels sang, it is written;
trumpets proclaimed His birth.
The stable, manger, where He lay
brought many to Him in love.
In the distance a Star was waiting
as God watched from above.

SUNRISE

Early morning prayers enlighten me

in laughter, joy...in sorrow.

The sun is covered in mist.

Is that a sign?

Streaks of clouds move across it

in a wind that blows intermittently.

Angels kiss each blade of grass

creating dew and growth.

Our Father's love embraces us

while bringing inner peace

to those who want it or need it for life.

He offers us beauty and strength.

He offers Himself.

I Can

One foot at a time.

Move forward.

What is wrong?

You can do it, can't you?

Focus on something...

the tallest tree in the forest.

One rain drop.

Impossible?

You have the power,

only you have the courage.

One foot at a time.

IT IS...

Days of mist.

Days of fire.

Days of bliss like no other.

Days of frost.

Days of loss.

Days of cost like no other.

Days of light.

Days of dark.

Days of fight like no other.

Days of hate.

Days of love.

Days of fate like no other.

Days of play.

Days of rest.

Days of work like no other.

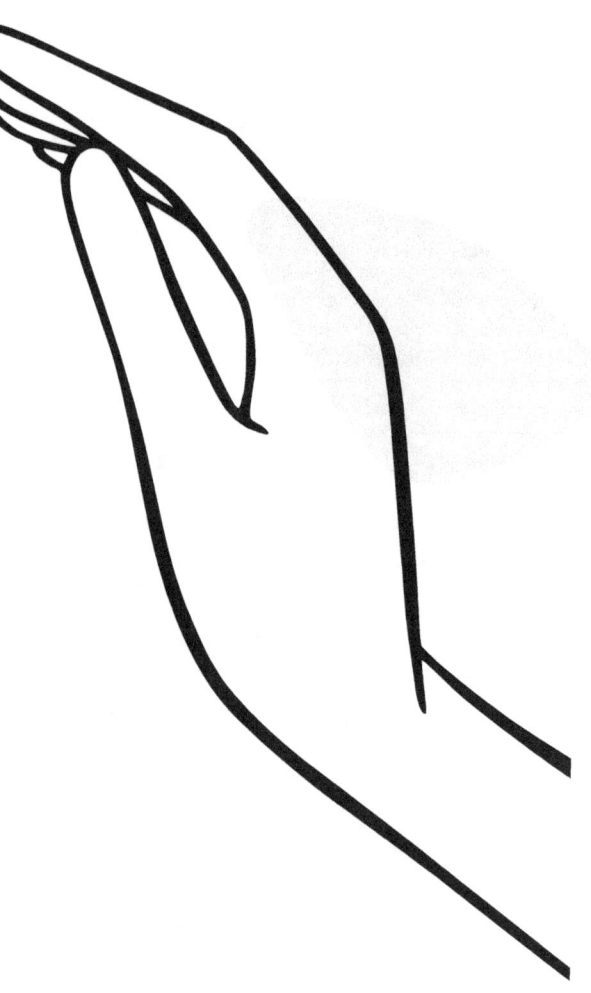

Pups

Dogs at the door, crying or barking
to make a good run 'round the place they know.
Run like the wind in warm, sunny weather.
Run through the snow digging holes as they go.
Jumping and playing, their life is a blast.
They're rescues letting go of their terrible past.
The heartaches, the bruises endured over again
are gone... they are loved and no longer in pain.

Am Here...

Stand aside, the Minister is here.

He sings a Psalm with his people,

his loving flock,

for he is the keeper for the Father.

A Minister,

a listener

of life toward Eternity.

He is always reaching out,

for he is the keeper of their dreams.

The Minister,

who writes his prayers with God,

sensing their passions, love, guilt, regrets

to give them inner peace.

For he is the keeper for the Father.

THE STORY

There we were
bathed in moonlight,
bodies glistening drops of gold.
Arms entwining,
lips just touching,
we never thought we could be so bold.
Sweet wind blowing soft against us,
the sun moves up another time.
Tears unshed we hold each other
loving... loving makes you mine,

ANOTHER TIME

I spent my childhood at Grandmother's home.

A tar paper shack and a hundred acres to roam.

The old wooden floor in the kitchen was spotless

with a table and bowl to pump water and then

a wood stove for cooking, don't touch it again!

There was a rope to the outhouse in summer or winter,

that you hung on to so tight or get lost in the night.

Jack Pines grew thick around a very large garden,

that she worked with a hoe in the early sun,

watching small children who loved to run...

SNOW DAZE

Warm clothes, boots and mittens too,

snow's so high it will bury you!

Shovels out...can't keep up.

Snowplows coming. No! Please stop!

Kids are warm. Their snowman's tall,

they dig a hole-watch out, don't fall!

Yeah! Got my skis and the old snowboard

but the snow's too deep, we can't go down, so!

We'll build a fire with sticks and logs...

grab the marshmallows and hot dogs.

It's cold out here in snowy weather

but bring a blanket, let's get together!

MEMORY

From college to church.
From home to the cottage.
Planting white pine,
felling a tree.
Building a road,
stopping for tea.
From counseling in love
and offering support,
building a Hospice,
to writing reports
on the passage of time,
the passage of life...
From home to the hospital
and back again
for the kidney, the heart...
good 'ol defib.
Now I know you'll live.

CHILDREN...

There is a box by that big old tree,
the one that holds fine sand, you see.
Castles were built with love and care.
I can almost see you there.
It seems you've grown away from me,
with little hands that played and shared...
I see an adult standing there!
The toys and trucks are still in play
by young grandchildren every day.

REFLECT

I sit in my favorite pew loving the peacefulness.

Stain-glass windows reflect the beauty

of colors in the glass and the scenes of Jesus' life.

Glory in itself.

Parishioners and visitors arrive little-by-little,

ushered in with friendliness and caring.

The organist takes her place to begin her masterpiece

for the morning, as the choir stands to sing the opening song.

The pastor walks in smiling and singing,

Thanks, prayers and joy at the same time.

I'm Coming!

Sometimes you just know when the last sunset comes.

It is etched in your mind as it fades.

You think back and smile at moments of happiness.

You let go of times of extreme sadness.

This is the next adventure. You will keep what is good...

Victory!

IT IS...

Anything I thought of you is just a moment in time.

Only a straight line...

Easier said than done.

Anything I hear from you was too hard to analyze,

so, let's just finalize...

Easier said than done.

I dealt with what I saw. You made it into law.

Now I realize...

Easier said than done.

Anything I felt from you I let it die in time.

I found no grace in you...

but easier said than done.

BYE...

It's appropriate, don't you think
to sit awhile and talk.
Maybe take a walk- we're on the brink...
for in a moment like this time is gone.
We'll say good-bye. It won't take long.
Life will go on, as it always does.
I wish you happiness. I wish you love...

ANOTHER TIME...

Ah, the luck of the draw in life!
What is the burden I shoulder?
It seems to be equal to war or strife,
and makes me a little colder.

I move through a day with desire
reaching out with hand and heart.
If being human would be any harder,
then life and I should part.

Just who am I anyway?
The secret is in my soul...
If I could tell you, what would you say?
Yes, life does take its toll.

Moment-by-moment, day-by-day
in my mind's eye I see.
that life is in heaven, maybe on earth!
The luck of the draw is in me.

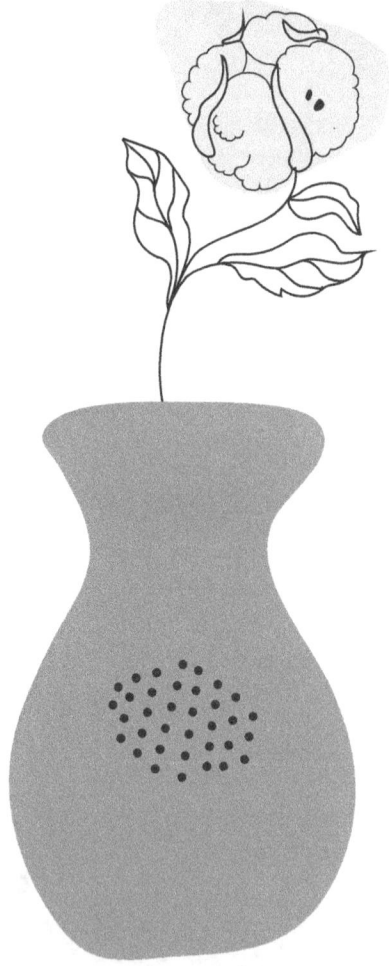

MIND'S SONG

I've always known you,
since my birth love.
I've always known you, my dear.
You weren't by me,
you couldn't see me...
I always knew you were near.
I was young then. So very young then.
I already knew you, though we hadn't met.
I had never seen you,
or talked to you. And yet...
The time has passed, dear.
so many years, dear.
I've always known you; you see.
I'm by your side, for you I long.
You just can't feel me...
you are my song.

A Love...

I stand on a high hill looking down into the valley.

Nothing is moving. It's so still.

The air holds the heat.

Under sunlight and shadows a slight breeze below moves grasses.

I kneel down and marvel at the wondrous sight I see.

My buckskins are worn from day-to-day living.

My hat is leather and old, with a band and a feather

that floated through the air to me.

I grew up in these hills as a child and I will die here as a man.

A man who loves to breathe the fresh air of early morning.

The sun is hovering, coming to an end...

My horse moves toward me. It is time to go home.

Again...

Each of us will celebrate in our own way,

the birth of our young Lord, Jesus...

We'll walk this path each day.

In light or darkness, He is always there,

we raise our voice to Him in prayer.

Jesus will grow in Spirit to teach us how to live,

to help each other hand-in-hand, and how to forgive.

Sunday Fellowship

Coffee together,
a natural bond

between Pastor,
Church Family and friends

in the fellowship Hall
at tables so long

enjoying coffee and donuts
as the morning moves on...

and I know Jesus attends.

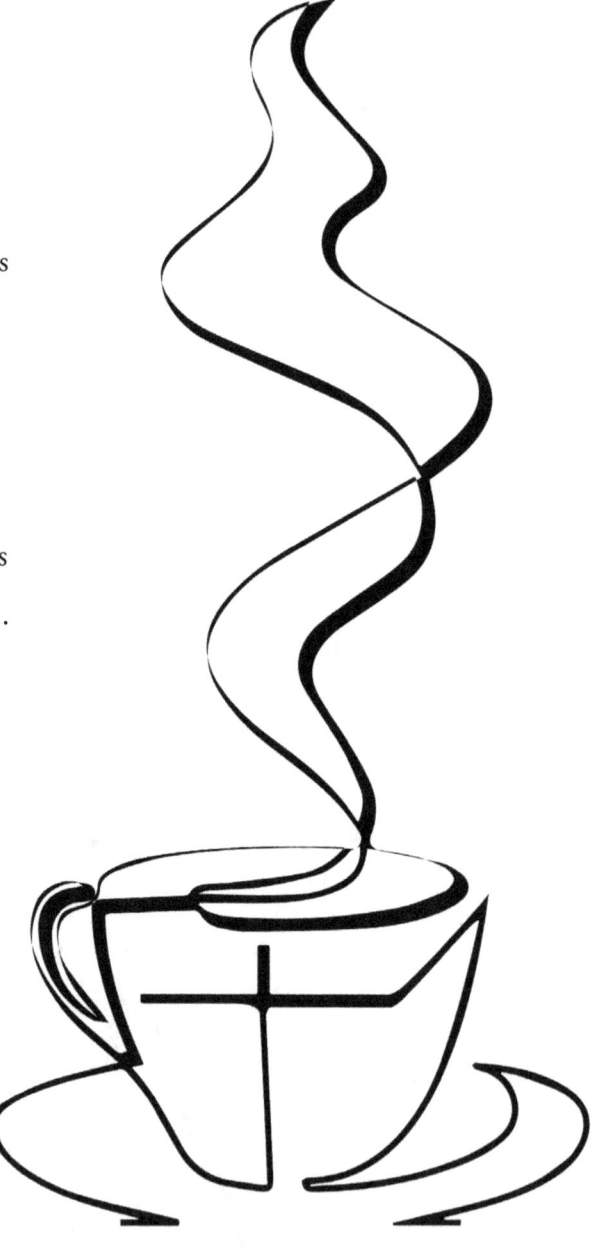

THE WALK

We walk together down the aisle toward the altar.

Do we

walk alone?

No. He is walking by our side.

He knows how we feel...

the emotion we feel in church.

I enjoy every minute of these feelings

that began in early childhood

and grew to what they are today.

When you spend that much time singing

to God and understand why,

He suddenly belongs to you and you to Him.

How special is that?

JESUS

We retreat to the comfort and warmth

of a fire in the coolness of night.

Jesus finds His warmth in the arms of His mother

from the hay he was resting on under the Star's

Light, illuminating the small family.

God's Work, Jesus Birth. Our Necessity.

To Love

I will cherish you
even if you are unattainable.
I desire you
with deep longing;
physically,
spiritually,
intellectually.
I want to caress you
with passionate abandon,
making you feel a
closeness that will not
come your way again.

Peace...

Enter the Church

in mystery.

Christ is present.

Hymns echo softly in the stillness -

compositions for the soul.

Lingering bodies seem to blend into

streams of light from

stained glass windows,

touching the altar,

bread and wine,

as it has for centuries.

The faithful have been called

to pray in solitude,

reawakening the Spirit within,

experiencing the love of our Lord.

COME...

Entering the forest at dawn,
I stand alone on a pine-needled path
hardly breathing, outstretched arms
reminiscent of our Christ.
The sunrise and beams of light
race downward in the sudden heat
of the day...
Silently I cry out at the feeling
of exhilaration within as a
quick breath suspends me with
the freshness of God's creation.
Oh, that everyone, everywhere
could experience in unison this
illumination of the Spirit.

WORKAHOLICS

Well, dear Lord. What do you want from us now?
You can't seem to leave us alone, to do our thing,
whatever that is. You are always pushing for more,
wondering why we aren't content to do
something! Sometimes it's hard to make you
happy and just relax for a minute. Well, after
running to and fro for you, caring for people,
saving children, holding hands of
those dying, we do appreciate being able to
sit with you and meditate. Your work is never
done Master, we know. The quiet times are
precious.

The thing about our Lord is He is behind you
all of the time! He will walk right on your
heels to do His bid. Actually, in the end
we do save or help many of His people.
 If it doesn't work out right, He isn't angry
with you...He prays. He goes and picks up
whomever needs Him and brings them home.
There are times to rejoice.

But for a Moment...

A warmth brings me to the fireside.

Your warmth brings me to you.

Your sweet breath fills me with life,

and I am brought close to your heart.

There is no resistance,

our arms are open in love...

not for love alone, or only a fleeting moment,

but for each other, always.

We will not be separated

for our time is before us, one and the other...

A sense of movement, a turn of the head,

a thought, and we find one another.

We are one.

It's Lovely?

"I'm hungry, hungry, hungry..."
echoes across the land.
Who is going to feed us or
give us a helping hand?
The farmer stands amidst his field
where a digger marks the grave
of yields that have been buried
by a bureaucracy so brave...

For if the farm is dead
and only a few exist,
on those few farms we cannot subsist -
and if corporations buy those farms
watch the price of bread jump out-of-bounds!

The farmer says there will be no food,

only the taste of fear -

fear of life and fear of death...

(eat that prayer the Bishop sent

'cause we can't afford to pay the rent!)

Do you think this poem's a myth?

"I'm hungry," will be the cry you hear,

for someone has to pay

for the many losses of farms

in the lovely U.S.A.

heart close to me,

as this music in the air sings.

I play music for you
You dance as my fingers touch strings.
I feel your heart close to me,
as this music in the air sings.

Memories of love, of caring in the early morning light.

my loving dogs chase a leaf

then turned to chase each other

as soon as they hear, "Treat?"

Oh, they loved their mother…

I love morning coffee

as sun rays touch the dew,

and morning birds are singing

building nests anew

CHRISTMAS POETRY

In Minnesota
Christmas winds blow.
Snow covers everything.

Christmas trees
sparkle in the moonlight.
Memories hang between branches.

Geese fly sharing their song.
Church doors open wide.
God's gift has arrived...Jesus.

CHRISTMAS AGAIN...

There is one thing I know,

the sun dipped down low

and darkness swept through the sky.

The moon cast its glow

on the great Star below

showing Joseph where Mary would lie.

Heavenly angels did pray

on that joyous day

when Jesus was born with a sigh.

God's breath in the wind

gently blew over Him,

giving Jesus His newborn cry.

A Christmas Thought...

Beneath the Hunter's moon
leaves fall and dance.
A river flows wildly
in anticipation.
Jesus is coming.
Church bells ring out
Thanksgiving blessings
in the season's first snow.
A glow touches the trees,
rocks and hilltops.
Angel's sing. God rejoices.
Jesus is here to bring comfort
to our soul.

Another Christmas

Life changes constantly,
but one thing hasn't changed.
The birth of Jesus our Savior
and His story throughout the ages.

The Christmas tree is up - six feet plus three.
Family and friends have arrived...
we hear their joyful glee!

The ornaments are out. Each one will put
theirs on the tree...
sitting by a blazing fire
with our memories to be.

CHRISTMAS

Beautiful soft snowflakes for Christmas.

Snowmobiles make the last round before
heading home to celebrate the birth
of God's descendant, Jesus.

He has arrived!
Jesus is lying in a manger watching,
waiting, seeing all in the warmth
of the land.

A BIRTH

Again, we celebrate the birth of Jesus

through His story,

through paintings of Mother and Child.

Through the ages with the creation

of His music to the end of time.

Our Savior, Our Messiah

who taught us to love, to help the poor,

all children...

It is Christmas.

We show our love for Him always.

CHRISTMAS

We sit at the table waiting for Christmas cookies
to turn brown. The recipe is explicit.
Glancing out the window a beautiful red Cardinal
sits at a feeder, nodding to us in thanks.
Flying low, a flock of geese skim the treetops,
their lovely call echoing through the coldness.
Looking towards the back yard I count eight deer
of all sizes munching on a dried blueberry bush for
dessert. We thank all of our wildlife for their visits
Now, Jesus is coming...

About the Author

Judith Kay Jacobs was born in Bemidji, Minnesota on March 14, 1942. The family moved to Fergus Falls, Minnesota in 1945. Judy began reading at five years old. She began writing At 23 and is still writing At 82. Judy has worked in many capacities at Grace United Methodist Church plus enjoying music as a handbell soloist. She was also church secretary at St. James' Episcopal Church for 16 years. In between, she enlisted in the U.S. Army and is a veteran. Judy and her late husband, Franklin, had four children: Bethany, Todd, Jeff and Sue plus many grandchildren: Kayla, Mariah, Alex; grandchildren Keagan, Jasmine, Ava, Maddie, Alexus and Blade, to whom this book is dedicated.